AF887068

Jargon 87

THE GARDEN PROSPECT
(Selected Poems)

THE GARDEN PROSPECT

(Selected Poems)

PETER YATES

The Jargon Society
1980

Certain of these poems have previously appeared in *Open Places, Arts in Society, Poetry Los Angeles I, Coastlines,* and *Prairie Schooner. Epitaph for Lorine Niedecker* first appeared in *Epitaphs* for *Lorine,* The Jargon Society.

Library of Congress Catalog Card Number: 79–83559

ISBN 0–912 330–41–4 (cloth)
ISBN 0–912 330–42–2 (paper)

Design by Jonathan Williams

Silverpoints by Susan Moore

Printed by Heritage Printers, Inc.,
Charlotte, North Carolina

Distributed by Gnomon Distribution,
P. O. Box 106, Frankfort, Kentucky 40602

CONTENTS

INTRODUCTION

Peter Yates wrote poetry all his life after his 17th year, and at times it was his principal occupation in a life full of occupations, yet he published little—one short book, *A Smaller Poem Book*, in 1946, a group in *Poetry Los Angeles* which he helped edit, and a scattering of poems in magazines. He seemed to have visualized publication of a collection eventually and from time to time made collections of his work, but he did not pursue the matter. Thus though widely recognized for his work in music and criticism, he is generally unknown as a poet.

A part of this was his growing preoccupation with music and aesthetic ideas which took up more and more of his time. There was also his recurring dissatisfaction with the possibilities of poetry as generally written in dealing with the real problems of experience. There was, further, his recognition that the type of poetry he felt called upon to write was too idiosyncratic, too against the modes of the times, in a way too personal, to gain much acceptance. So he wrote as he saw fit and left the matter at that. He was always a nonconformist—even against the conformity of nonconformity. He was one who would go his own way.

Yet he began as a poet, and throughout his life poetry lay at the center of what he did—the acute sense of inner language, the sense of the tangential and plural possibilities inherent in words. This reflects in his prose but shows more clearly in his poetry. He wrote to fit his thinking which was questioning, searching, full of play and crosslights, radical in its depth, paradoxical. There is lightness in it and much humor, but these are part of the questioning. Underneath there is the depth, the profound engagement. He had a singular skill of devotion—family, friends, people and things he loved. But he had also a massive integrity and scope of mind, and had a horror of the facile. He would earn his insights.

This is what gives his poetry its particular quality and force. It is his own. In music, self-taught, he considered himself primarily an amateur and brought to music the freshness of approach and directness of response of the true amateur. Similarly in poetry his approach was immediate and out of his love of it. He early, from Hopkins, discovered what could be done with the sonnet and built it to a rich and innovative expressiveness. Later he worked in freer forms both in metric and cadence, and, still later, experimented with non-linear arrangements in an attempt to develop a new way of verse. He relished jarring and clashing rhythms, the ambush of normal expectations, the twisting of form to open new vistas, the ironic or enhancing juxtaposition of contraries. He would even attempt, in one of his poems to Stravinsky, the rigor of working in double and reversed acrostic which became the scaffolding for a noble and penetrating poem. But it is perhaps in the strictly controlled freedom of the long *Lecture: On the Rocks* that his medium is at its best—subtle, playing at the edge of prose, far-ranging in its rhythmic as well as other inventions, iridescent with many searching pluralities, charged finally with the presence of the angel.

This is not poetry too easily come to nor, once come to, easily forgotten. Following one of his favorite dicta, it is as it is. He once spoke of his poetry as an "act of statements, each including, or it may be in another poem, its contradiction," and these statements are deeply rooted in living as he saw it—his family, his friends, his beloved garden, doubts and searchings and acceptances, tributes and celebrations. He wrote as he saw fit, but his seeing had unusual scope and freedom.

In arrangement this book of selections is roughly chronological with the poems from *A Smaller Poem Book*, some of them dating back to 1932, first, followed by poems from the 1950s and early 1960s centered on *The Garden Prospect* series, and a concluding group of those written after 1964. The selection has been made with a view to indicating the full round of his thinking and style. In the work of preparing it I have had much help from Melissa Blake Levitzky, a long-time friend of both of us; from Frances Mullen Yates, Peter's wife; and from Eleanor Bender. The task has been made easier, if saddened, by recollection of the man himself, one of immense energy, courage and generosity, who illuminated everything he touched.

PEYTON HOUSTON

THE GARDEN PROSPECT

(Selected Poems)

I. From *A Smaller Poem Book*

WHAT WAS SO FAIR IS DARK AND VAST

What was so fair is dark and vast,
No wrinkle crossed,
That abstract.

The delicate, particular
Throat is undone:
Cry in the corridor;
Give room.

Grasp and scope and clasp
Made to be wooed:
Tell the children body is now their food.
There is no real left

But dark and vast
As this still air
Where breath nor breathing is.

WEDDING SONNET

This browned sod, when it was turned up alone
Out of its lawn, this branch broken by the wind,
And this blown feather:
Or whether the falling sinned,
Or whether
Man being divided was therefore alone,
The fall fated; and the intellectual mind
Sensing the rhythm becomes inexorably lone;
Form fails, and with the clarity of one blind
He feels and cannot see limits he has known alone.

Inexclusive, the sod in the earth greens like
Within the leafy tangle the branch bursting,
And the hawk a feathering, a comet:
Dear sweet soul, my soil, oh, be all like
This earth at the green season,
A thirsting
Searching beyond reason
Life, rhapsody without surface and without limit.

IF I HAVE FAILED IN BEING TALL

If I have failed in being tall
And am not anything at all,
You cannot say that I am broad,
For that would be to measure God.

If I am made of nothing worth
The measuring of the seed in earth,
I can be neither plant nor root.
What I must offer is a fruit

Which never grew on vine or tree,
A name, a shape, a taste like me,
Bearing no history and no past,
Present only in your hands' grasp.

Make of this then without excuse
A real, perennial in use,
A man, having authority
By your hands' touch to live before I die.

Our children's calling ornaments
Harmonious unison of days
Sharpening with shriller voices
Music that's enlarged by discord.

Hear the coloring: bright noises,
Dark against, a small lament
Of the babe's peculiar discant:
Our own home's music, love embraced.

BEING AMONG FRIENDS TAMED STRANGERS

Being among friends tamed strangers not
ungratefully warrants a belief in
if they weren't we would try to persuade them

What they are we have been and loving
cherish in them being not well founded
presuming to borrow of their needing

Make in ourselves the moral we expended
like a child wakening to the dreamed toy it hasn't
out of the love and luminous gratitude sleeping

What not to expect is wisdom enemy of bright-eyed
innocence in being needless
sleeping or waking without need of gift or hope

To the very inward curving upon itself
stilled as no night rode with no sword no wooden horse

FOR THE BIRTH OF A THIRD CHILD

Thanks, friend, the child is well,
Strong of a strong line, mother and father in him:
Let the history that shapes in him make history.

Thanks, friend, for pain and prayer,
That have made and will direct him as you will:
And let him too have portion in pain and prayer.

Do not take him: make him: for in him the future,
Asleep before struggle, leads him against our goodness.

Son, break, make and cherish, but do not fear:
This mad world maddens many of countenance;
The fleshed round shrivels in despair;

And many that would be, many that are great hide from it:
Cruelty is their first tomb; they perish out of use:
Here is my soil, dig it; water, drink it; breathe my air.

FROM ANNIVERSARY

Globed in the corneal dark of space
Beyond the color of the sky
The mountains with the desert lie,
The formula a compass trace:
  I can see with a fish's eye;
            I fly.

And in that nerve and in that brain
No vestiges of me begin;
My existence is not seen,
Thus reality is plane.
  I have my sky in a telescope:
            I hope.

There an incorporeal graveness
Cannot know my little purpose
Starling-like in separate chirpness
At the margin of forgiveness:
  These stars inform a rooftop galaxy,
            Here me,

Who contain within this globed,
Mailed, transparent envelope,
All a man can know of scope,
Job's tenderness in Satan robed,
  More than science, more than beast,
            A host.

If my power is unseen
As secret-creeping in the groin,
As nervous impulse in the brain,
You, who must rule, shall be the queen,
  Throned on the farther side of light,
            My night.

Dear one, religious is this straining
When with our bodies spaces join,
And faces do not guard the line
Of star-crossed essences combining:
   Hold, that our silence be not blind,
         Me blind.

The prophecy is plain
Upon faith's premises
Hope will defeat its nemesis,
The cynic's hand sprout grain.

BEAUTY, THAT WILD BEAST, LIKE A MOUSER PLAYING

Beauty, that wild beast, like a mouser playing,
This in the garden and among wild shoots,
Green, above the tuber-wisdom of the roots,
Brown, and beauty paw-patting like a kitten playing,
Chasing in and out above the regular roots:
In the young age, when the head of my heart is greying.

This revelation happens before the evening:
You, who are in the revival of every hour
Younger, the root of my green, gay bloom and livid flower
Of eagerness, stiffening and lifting to mature desire,
Need, rather, I think, for where the passions were
I need you, as the savage needs his god,
A physical dupe, sacred to me as the Hebrew leavening
Or unleavening, the essence sweeter than the act,
consuming, of the daily bread.

WHY SHOULD YOU, ARTIST, WHY SHOULD YOU NOT DARE

Why should you, artist, why should you not dare
The final agony: you are not wanted!
Bear it in the elevation of the mind;
And, if you cannot, with the spirit . . .

Rig a technique, rig out a new technique
For reason—reason is dead, the intuitive
Daylight dims in the carved halls. Rig a spirit
For a reason, like a scaffolding, or a fresh light will . . .

Why, aren't you paid for it! What gulden guild,
Artist, pays you for a living? Rig a new technique.
The invincible, the invincible will—decorator—
Out of old furnishings set us up a discreet order.

And the living will remain with Blake, Bach, Angelo,
Beethoven, saints and prophets who dared that men should live.

A TWELVE-TONE STATEMENT OF POPULAR OPINION IN REGARD TO ARNOLD SCHOENBERG AND HIS MUSIC

If it were not for that, we could love you
Like anything—anything it were; if not
For that we like, love you.

We're for it; we could love you
Like anything, not that, if love
Were like—if for that
Could anything: it, not you, we love not.

Anything, we're for it: you like it if that
We love not like that.
If anything could, you were for it; we
Could love you for that.

Not anything like it! We were, if anything.
That you love we could like it,
If for anything, that you like, love, love.

FOR CHARLES IVES

If there is left, men's God, in the world one single man
To speak of you and be friend, too many words
Cannot hide you or deny you for that man.
He will be like a history when it is lived,
Not yet made faith, and in him you in him;
The greens of leaves, the blues of seas will be no more tangible,
  no more real.
He will come up like spring; in winter men will live in memory
  of him;
And death shall be forgetting, even as one man has forgotten
  spring:
This God who inhabits words and works in men
And who is real in the person, real and final as the speech
Of one who, feigning, cannot feign to feign;
This real enduring stout truth's counterchange:
Death does not affirm and cannot fail
Him in whom living is a part in being.

JAMES JOYCE

The durable integrity of a man made great
By it, the enduring finality of a gesture all man made
Fertile, as the seed returns to seed,

Round, or as the word that makes the mind come back,
Compel creation, whom I do not know:
Do you attend?

The life, then, in the man, or mind, or making
Integrate:

And if so in the silverpoint one see divine,
In tone divine,
In pencil, who is it draws then?

Writes: war, my many many mine!
What can you do, offering
No further sanctity but to live to die.

MEDITATION ON LEONARDO DA VINCI

And the thoughts turn towards hope: thoughts
Incompletely pursue hope towards one being,
And of diverse arts make one doing.

The finch in his cage, the goldworker's room—
Hope will come through: freedom is the freeing:
Duty will make its round—in ignorance of the world will
starve pursued.

As a work is no man's end but before his life
Is freeing; in pure freedom finds neither pressure nor good.

Last night and first day celebrate
One New Year, every hour in the round
Of waiting that each new time deliberates.

Tell me if anything was ever done
Like the form of water, a plait, tendrils,
And then freshing, fraying the like motion.

THE SNAKE

it is the little beautiful unseen snake which kills,
the bright asp and the coral; it is the little snake
coiled in the sun's heart, and the little coiling snake
about the ankle, where the flesh heats the wrapped coils:
teeth sink in warm flesh; then the flesh fails
and light feet trip; it is the sucking asp of the full breast, that
snake,
that little dangling in the bosom chill, that sharp-toothed
snake:
it is the little brilliant snake in the head which kills:

legless and spinal, ornamental worm,
in hope's color deceiving, camouflage of the sun,
you wriggling fear and calm, envenomed cone—
Pharaoh and death's bone:
FEAR, foul when most gorged and when most gorged undone:
crawling terror, maw with jagged gape,
pliant copious belly, eye, unlidded ache,
jointed in parody of bestial form
freezing the ape:
the poisonous fear I cannot flee, you snake!

BE NEAR ME NOW. THE HOUR'S CHANGE GROWS STRANGE

Be near me now. The hour's change grows strange.
Each evening prefaces a haunted morning.
Each moment history ends. Thus history ends.

And yesterday is piled against the sun:
Even today darkness, darkness is begun;
Tomorrow yields no plan.

Tomorrow is.
Against this certain all false premises
Are true, and worth's a pocketful of pennies.

Be near: the day's, the night's act will not change.
Love having been will win: you and I know it.
We have planted a good seed: this soil will grow it.

Sweet and ripe will be the fruit,
And frustrated is the weed;
In our hope love nourishes
   Life that will endure love's need.

AND CAN WE TAKE FOR GRANTED EXCELLENCE

And can we take for granted excellence,
Can we accept, and choose that fault to distinguish
What was in the man a making, is that like a fault in him?

Wisdom works in ways wide as a meadow,
A hedged squareness, only here's a stream
That slopes a side: elbows, and grass grows this side of the
  stream.

Elbows, and what's ugly in an elbow?
Isn't it being beauty in an elbow as it's seen?

Would you wing the wild bird and wind out
The cycle: dying, he will remember, is an end.
Sentences end: it's like a book of paragraphs.

The hunters kill living, kill to be alive;
Through a curved elbow the straight message springs,
Wings the wild beauty, rounds the dying: yet day does not
  end.

SURGE THE IDEA DOWN THE PAGE

Surge the idea down the page:
It is one thought like that; and the image
Creeps in the mind womb, blind, to meet its image.

There's a reaction to all artifice,
A delight in being knowing more than pleasure
The living measure, better than tinsel or ice.
Measure that's a phrase in words or music,
Shape to remember, if a rule a menace,

Or an erect grizzly—danger of the claws!—
Hunting's more than pleasure; the live threat to life
Beats finger-count, the esthetic target-practice:
Well, it's a wise man wills it, if he can.

The rules repose, and the rare purple gentian,
Common naked seen one time, not a flower but a rite,
Assumes all nature, knows, in a breathing instant,
all one time.

WHAT DISASTER, GOD, HAVE YOU PREPARED FOR ME

What disaster, God, have you prepared for me
To destroy what I have made—a trembling of the flesh?
In what green field, what air, upon what rock, what sea;
When will some night not waken: when will some day not end?

Who will go out and come not back again?
Strike now; take now. Fear is the enemy.
Pain met is courage known. There is no plan,
No hope, no assurance can hide me.

Then by what faith can I assume that fate
I will fail not? Rather the good grey days,
Quiet nights of stars unnamed, the sweet grass pasturage.

But it will come yet, even to the innocent,
The knife out of the book, one ritual sentence:
Truth has been met, even by the innocent.

POET'S CORNER

For Emily Dickinson

1

Make me a coronet
And set it on me gaudy;
My tomb is in the Abbey
With folk I haven't met.

The crowning of my king
Is a wise man's party,
With conversation hearty,
And everything . . .

Most ceremonially
Contrived.
The nation sent
Cloth of gold cerement
To prove the noble lived.

The gift's a gift in vain
In the grandchild's reign.

2

Eloquent imbecile,
Parsifal—what
Said the fool, Simple Simon,
In buying a hat?

To keep out the weather,
To keep his brains in,
He'd need to be given
Gold—a crown with a brim.

3

Creation's a custom
we have, as to rule

The imperial portion.
What excuse for a fool

Who has it and will not,
Or if he would, can't
Prefer the investments
Of dullards to scents?

4
Heine, Mozart,
Schubert, kleinchen,
Old Bach's wife's on the town:
We'll throw a shady party
And ask Jack Skelton down.

You inconsiderable fellows
And empty to the state,
Windy by-words, good for bellows
To the fire of your fate!

Send the word to Villon,
Keats, Sam Johnson, Coleridge, get
All the world's worthless worthies;
We'll have a benefit.

Tolstoi, Goethe, Voltaire greet us;
The charade, *Success*, is Shaw's:
Then drain our old deservings
In the cellarage of applause.

5
Blake sing a prayer for me;
Then Emily Brontë
Speak me another one;
Then Emily Dickinson
Breathe; and thy will be done.

6

Here the electric light,
Madame, defies the slight of decency;
You would not do well here
With this bulb in your garden.

Neon crescent and the fake
Ephemeral galaxy:
You would not do well here, Madame,
With this bulb in your garden.

My skyline is a black
Obscure stage-setting for the real
Unlighted, even the moon
Too near.

There I see you, Madame,
Like a hump on that mountain,
Moving, out of the ribs of the world,
Against this incandescent universe,

Whose light will go out, too,
With the electric bulb and the neon,
When the real pinprick of reality,
Garnished with angels,
Reaches the enduring ages of the fixed stars.

Even then the electric light,
The crescent neon, and the reminiscent candle
Will remain, if we have made them,
As you your perceived moments,
Fixed with the eternal.

II. From *The Garden Prospect*

THE GARDEN PROSPECT

This is to be the orangery, and the clipped yew beyond.
All the forms have been revised, the hedges trimmed in line.
Sleek and with sharp ears the wakened owl, fearfully blinking,
queries of the undergrasses. The butterfly
uncoils his honey-lacquered tongue.
His beauty feeds on the ripe green of my garden.
It is the end of summer, the plants gone to weed.
Here I shall light a fire and from my window
see the maples blazing and then after snowfall
attend bleak winter and watch whither spring renews.

File me in the pages of your book of
precious love. File me under Sleek and Jaded.
File me under Not Much Longer, Not a Good Insurance Risk.
After me the revision, after me no more accountability.
Set me in the direction of a retired man headed south,
leaving the top of a table rapidly filling
with incongruous, documentary grandchildren,
wife-eyed, father-featured.
I can see Europe at last and care not.

Set me, darling, on the one road homeward, darling, beyond the no returning.
I have heard enough and made my decisions.
If it is of any consequence, I have signed in and signed out,
paid and am now drawing my insurance pretty penny.
I have been a good citizen and marked time.
Began bold as Browning and end eerily an existentialist.
Whatever it is, it is of my time.
My youth a broken rapier, my maturity an imaginary mistress,
my age a transfer to yesterday's bus.

The Dinosaur at Quitting Time

I have visited in the racing cities
conceived by peace out of autonomy; have stripped in military
   offices.
I have known that history was being made while I was busy
and believed, crawling between sheets, that one way or another
   I might make it.
Am I also an exception to the rule that nothing happens
except accidents, fiction of an imaginary lust
to be past and present at once?.
                                        After me, what delusion?

Before me, I am told, the lichen, the dinosaur consorted
in the way of nature, and what went on went on
changing. I have made my pile and will lay on it.
Raising my extension I dial a number, and nobody answers.
The office is vacant. It is after quitting time.

The Cast Eye at History

Can it be that in another century and place
there was calm, order, method?
                                        O rapidly the rose
                                        is twining up the trellis
That a great queen between unsatisfactory
remorses diligently managed, that a king
was not an ass? I fear we clothe them more kindly
than their courtiers, who saw the body undressed.
      O the queens who slept with kings, what did they know
      of political economy; and the kings who slipped from queens,
      what could they know
      of equalitarian humanity?
The pitiless philosophers philosophized
by the stream of the moment, solitary and more strait
than rulers, product of the three ways meeting

of less regally bedded but more aristocratic genes.
Is it there that thought and therefore tragedy begins?
    O a dude descending a staircase
    or a prize beef-bull at stud . . .
What do you know! What do you know?

I commend me to my ancestors, I commend me
to my great-grandchildren and strangers,
and to theirs and relatives by marriage,
a bourgeois socicty of cousins.
I commend me to be examined by those shrubbery moralists,
historians, biographers, myth-makers.
Here I deplore and categorize their inventions.
Nomad garrulities chute, spitting and rumbling, past my hedges.
These days preserve nobody; nobody preserves letters.
Documents, the pride of centuries, now have a term.
File me in the dead file, among the unappealed decisions.

The Laughter

Over there the little
female fountain I laughingly
mounted bronze in my garden
drily laughs at me.
A lizard creeps by the footstone.
Comedian and heir of reptiles,
which of us shall inherit my garden?
The windows have been washed clean.
All things that in their day shall come to seemliness
or crawling, yet few shall be seen through,
these reside in me.
                    And a little staircase upwards,
where I pause waving goodnight to the company,
may lead me to my bed.

The Wisdom

By what grimness unprovided
of celestial imaginings
do I turn to my garden? There
everything is fair, or may be, under the eye of the gardener.
Shall a book counsel, or an orange? Where is greater sweetness?
Will excitement turn me out or do me in?
Is there only wisdom for a wise man? I do soberly ask that
of the little bronze bird perching on the basket
of my bronze companion.
                                        Genius of affirmation,
is your smile meaningful? May I turn safely from mankind
to you? Did the hand of a master make you,
or a spoiler, a makeshift?
                                        Here, retired from my office,
in the house of my retirement, confronting my green lawn,
I am reduced to wondering and melancholy.
                                                        Work . . .
but enough of that; work—but satiety; work
has been the opiate I have consulted for my wisdom.

The Power

I who include the cosmos,
history, geology, who know the paths of the stars
and their nature that is not as men made them
but as men know them, I sit on my lawn
before autumn, between the orangery and the garden,
before winter which shall drive me in and enfeeble
the precious remnant of my light from afar off.
I summon electricity more certainly than the occult,
knowing that when I summon it will come
and that what I see by is not mathematics.
Latin will add no substance to my verses
nor Greek to my sophistry. Buddha will not explain the infinite.

If I go on my knees, I must fear to be superstitious,
but forlorn if I do not.
                                        I am reduced to cry to my light:
How far, how far you have brought us!
You who have led us through the red sea,
where is the desert ending?
                                        Is it you I should cry to . . .
or to a germination as precise as meaningless,
an order germinated in the good nature of a chemistry?
The procession of the religious, the philosophers,
sweeps silently by me and over their heads swarms of atoms
and beneath their feet no solid, and from their mouths
contradictions.
                              The pageant of a glorious destiny
eludes me like music, its reasoning like the voices of the fugues
Bach made who believed in one God.
I can do no better; and must that satisfy me
in my passion, in the quiet, comfortable garden
between the orangery and the clipped yew?

Must I shudder only and die. . .

The Pain

The pain of living, for the lives shut out from life,
is not less by the value of the best-sellers that console them.
The sick mind in its excrement crouches nearer God
than a good man at his sacrament.
And a man who is right before the eyes of the world
and justified by his contentment
defies charity and justice.
So be wrong. Be wrong!
But the good man justified in his contentment will say,
"I have earth and heaven."

Must I shudder and die . . .

The Denunciation

Each day
in eyes that cannot see
the sun dies again.
        In minds that dream
        Phaethon crosses,
        and the horses of the chariot of the sun
        are given names.
                In eyes that see
                nothing is visible but the equation
                of an order that succeeds.
        In the foreseeing
        imagination
        there is beginning
        and end, or progress
        or not, as the fit finds him.
In the rejecting
closed eye of the god-possessing
is the iron of virtue.

I shudder and die.

The Concluding in Prosperity upon a Roman Theme

It is time for dinner and for action.
Leave contemplating to the divinities of the garden.
Come, my friend, let us pull ourselves together
with a concoction of good liquor,
so that our appetite may be apt to the occasion
as our conversation to the presence of good women.
Leave the lizard, the dry fountain statue,
the clipped yew, and the rushed garrulities beyond,
all things questionable and disorderly.
                                                            Let us savor our ripe taste
at a good table, trusting in sleep without nightmare
and a wakening at morning.

THE HUMMINGBIRD

The hummingbird
in my garden ignores me
because I cannot bloom.

THE WHALE

So many excellent
poems, as poems:
   what have they
   to say

The whale in my garden
will not eat, it
does not fly, it
   cannot swim

That I report to you

THE SQUASH

I tire myself
I knot up my mechanic body
with labor, like a drug
because I don't need to!

Building my walls
assembling terraces of rock, heavily
laid together, for no purpose.
No one requires it of me.

I don't value the flowers,
the peach trees, the pumpkins
that will show there, for their fruits:
these are my ornate companions.

And at night I lie dreaming
of the great squash, throwing out his whiskers, creeping
up my terraces
when I'd much rather sleep.

But if I sleep I die
and my waking is precarious.
I fear to lie down among the cut green branches
side by side along my terraces.

I build a pyramid to myself
that none will admire, no one will observe in
this stone step my calculation,
bracing that wall my judgement.

And the rebellious greens,
the high dahlia, the fuchsia dropping purple race,
the acanthus pride, the coarse file of the squash
are my testimonial: we shall not survive summer.

Is it better to improvise
or carve a monumentum aere perennius
or to exchange verses until drunk
or defy the indifference of editors?

THE TERRACED GARDEN

When you come into my garden
you must come into my garden:
understand the sand pond,
survey the azaleas with a diligence
like theirs and say to yourself:
this man knows what he is doing;
it will never end with himself.
Was it doggerel or divinity
spoke out of Delphos?
a double-dealing, a little of both.

Now if a man offer an observation
on the scenery about him,
we may say: His imagination paints.
Or after a completed friction,
panting, his sensibility breathes words;
or if his heart be a singing,
we may say:
We were not with him in those well-used parts
where he lusted playing,
nor do we see or feel with his sighs.

All that he has known, imagine!
of all that he pretends
he may lose, leave:
or has he ever been there?
disgust, disillusion?
He may or not, nonchalantly
dissipating, puring,
emptying the amphorae

over a still waterless pool,
dissimulating or dispensing.

I do not walk in my
garden to be observed by neighbors
nor to be
there, silently myself meditating
philosophical eels
floating out of their bungholes
veiled in floating tropics.
I have planted in order these rocks,
aware,
among the pooled refractions of the leaves.

But my friend, my enemy, the sun
strikes cell and stirs all growth
like unto unlike, crisps, dries,
pricks
fruiting and to defect:
in my garden the curled leaf
droops and the shadeless
limbs lift gaunt-withered.
Under the white cumulus, green-
rivuleted like mountains the buds sweat.

Come, if you wish, upon
these terraces of shade and desert
proudly on the road of Pharaoh, erecting
his perennial flower, deathly
royal monument, enthralled
figure of robed caverns.

Transient among the patterned
caterpillars you will see me
on the terrace greenly sipping:
you may meet yourself visiting.

In my garden waking
to arts that will betray me
I waste in meaning
and with fame manure my talents.
Stripped, flayed, I am, ritually
disjointed and dismembered.
The muscles of the esoteric
maidens drum on my tense belly;
they feast on me,
they strip me of ripened fruit.

THIS MAN INTENDING GOOD

worked hard at what he did
doing no man wrong
and was ignored for that reason

The spoilers, takers
winners of places
outdoers of outdoers
outdid him in notice

Undid himself in
disdain and resentment
having mangled
the good in him

Shall posterity:
we know we know

One myth with angels

WHOEVER CANNOT BELIEVE THE GOOD

Whoever cannot believe the good
will of mankind inherit evil,
and whoever does so believe
conjures an approving devil.
Sweet sister Truth, do not let Faust hold your hand.
The man is all lies and science.

THE LONELY MAN

looks out the window and sees anybody
smiling, everybody
happy; the lonely man
looks out his window, and it's
nobody
nobody, nobody

The lonely man
looks out the window and sees anybody
like him, everybody
coming, going; the lonely man
looks out his window, and it's
anybody
not like him

Out of his window
the lonely man
sees everybody coming going
somebody, anybody;
the lonely man, that lonely man
looks out his window, and it's
everybody safely
inside
outside him

Everybody outside
anybody smiling
nobody needing
anybody inside; in a glass window
pane
that lonely
somebody smiling
happy, happy; and it's
looking
right through him

TO BREAK OUT OF MY PRIVY SKIN

To break out of my privy skin,
mock the mocker mocked within,
declaim upon the tree-foiled stage
forbidden youth, impotent age,
star-sung, a thrasher in a room;
and a thrasher beating bare
light antennae in the air.
Beauty, beauty born in vain
flattens at the window-pane,
turns within, again, and there
weaves nesting strands of greying hair.

Who would go outward must turn home.
Let him attack who has most room
to suffer with least need of rage.
Declaim the curses of the age.
Return the mocker mocked within
the passage of his privy skin.

MEDITATION:
Where one comes who will not come
(for Glanville)

In the heart of
God is a garden
for each alone
where no one comes

Where each tends
his garden lonely
waiting for the visitor
who sometime may come

In the heart of God's heart
in a desert
lost, horizonless
where no one comes

Infertile, imperfectible
in the heart of
each tends a garden
where the gardener may come

Farther and ever farther
from each presentness
the garden blooms:
each must wait who comes

ever as if unwanted
not to be answered
beside the pathway
where one may not come

I sit by the cup
of the flower
in my garden waiting
silentness that will come

When the questioning ends
the waiting
blooms in the heart
he need not come

Infertile, imperfectible
man cannot answer
need in his knowing
he cannot come

What I have been
I am not.
I am not what I may be
if he should come

He cannot need me:
without me
no needing:
then, he will come

I rest waiting
by the heart of the flower
in a desert in a garden
where God never comes

Confirmed after the event by Glanville's beloved Gregory of Nyssa: "And this is the real meaning of seeing God: never to have this desire satisfied."

IF A MAN CANNOT BUILD A NEW HOUSE
(A Message to Kenneth Rexroth)

Where shall I hasten to evade
this dutiful burden, being as I am
what time, persistence, and rough weather shape me?
If I take to the sea,
many are there drowned and dead
whom sweet singers call by name,
and others irony.
Robbers are on the land, and wars course
ravenously;
air is heavy with falling.
If all from responsibility are fled,
shaking their distraught heads wagging
against responsibility,
who will feed on cropped beards or summon
diviner voices by their barked calling?

If alone, disaffiliate, I believe that I evade
what I am, where I am,
uncommitted either to go or stay,
shall I escape where others cannot
or remain where no others remain?
Is nature for the solitary
without luxury?
Is not luxury the man's mark,
marble head, pillar of his temple?
If he abuse, does not luxury
luxuriate
in his decay?
I cannot within these shores be absent
from perilous luxury.

Saving the oceans do not swallow me

and robbers leave me possessed
and the constituency of the air is not
poisoned or tyrannized;
I cannot, myself,
myself I cannot evade.
Look! on the food-gathering shore, involute, a crabbed
specimen, heavily shouldering my ill-fitting
carapace or borrowed hut:
love nourished me, or I were not;
I set this against others' hatred.
Fugitive out of the waste and the mosaic
plowed contours:
passion houseled me, in commune;
the stone city is my attic past.
Tomorrow is for me today
in consequence of yesterday: unless
I build a new house above death,
invite mockers singing to my trees
and expect stools in my garden; unless
I am responsible in my presence.

If a man cannot build a new house,
anyone may despair.
                    That is my message.

MOZART

The cynic who in Mozart dwells
speaks in us from secret hells.
Mozart the child a cherub is
running with arms out to our bliss.
This radiance of piercing light
is Mozart, but behind is night.
In years a man but little more;
in wisdom never aged two-score;
in spirit a transfigured vision,
energic head of pure decision;
being like a wraith all wrapped around in
worlds the human is not found in:
yet not unlike, yet not unlike.
What in one tone an hour may strike
is new time and a new day's date.
Our salvation rings from that.

TO THE UNRESTING

Creative rest, night of the unceasing mind,
that, when the day dawns, darkens inward:
in silence, where to be content is to be empty;
to be empty, filled: restless achievement, pirating
an empire; to contemplate, an autobiography:
being at rest, inward within inward.

The cut stone does not move: to be released
it is to be drilled, chipped, flaked, hammered;
freed by an artifice, mannerless, without precedent.
And what is it to look like? Not, my boy, no, not like you!
Never was a Greek modeled by Phidias
but marble, sculptured marble, painting it then godlike
in the popular colors: the achieved was not a look-like.

It was make-work for the city, tax-supported,
subtled those high columns, hung the invisible high
battle of lapiths and of gods, part genius
of the city and part her unemployed. Where did
beauty creep in and at what rock-tumble
contemplation of the aging, neglected, captured, exhausted city?

To be at rest: it is to be a static eye,
empty and dreaming ceased, and behind these,
still, and behind, motionless; until the mechanic figure
cracks, and it is all one inward silence,
while the restless flesh accepts peace; as though the composite
of neurons and neutrons, the invisible nothing had been nothing uttered.

Yet of this, creative rest, night of faith, surety
of darkness, unprobeable, unproved
divinity of presence, not to be reckoned or like a sun captured
by ceaseless observings: no, no calculating mind
can enter that luminous theology or note
its zeros under parsecs, ever deeper into motive.

Out of this comes, not by chance, chance thought,
not by pride—which is to be, not enter, nought—
the one linking, to see under and within;
visioned grasping of the non-dimensioned; sign
that is an eagle and a message, revelation
and a calibration of the unmeasured; an in which was not.

For by this toehold, brushing my teeth, squatting,
to be comes in grasp, tool, quantum, to grind color and paint,
to sink a sharp rock in the pole's cleft
and throw it, that this theme will shape:
that measure, thus modeled, will command
to make the uncalculated, careless, accurate spring upward.

And afterwards to debate, contemplate,
no, not by chance, for the eye
thinks, hand sees darkness, the ear
erects abstract dimensions, the prickling
of the flesh tells of ghosts, the tongue—
oh, the tongue institutes cities and the lies men orate.

And so silence must be died for, punished
and died into. You know this silence is larger
than the noises men make. To be is to be disciplined.
Like a street accident chance happens.
The autobiography each one contemplates
has been restless with men and women, voices crying
and apologizing for the nonsense each bearing begets.

Parents, wife, husband, children, the gross
particularities under the flung mesh, entrapped
embarrassment in clothing, the encitement
of things wanting and unwanted: perdurable, unplanned
home, fled from by the silences,
where by day each is divided, at night violated, unmanned.

Each seeks rest before dying, to die living in the silence
of a seacoast uninhabited, of an island without tourists,
of a nation traditioned and unlawed,
of an idea within an idea without foemen,
unenemied silence, where the fawning
lion tongues like a cat the relaxed hand.

So to wrap this silence around us,
each one wearing silence, so to dance in the dance of fears
unterrified; to lie down each in silence and arise
like the lion wakening in Eden: it is to be abstract
in silence, as sexual and real in presence; to become
what each is not, being now what each one is.

The morning birds scattering their charted
cries utter an uncharted music, ever similar
within ears' range, breaking the black welcome,
aloof, of silently tormented sleep.
Waking, the day crows, the insisting
sunlight crowds into the dark cubicles the seeds.

And restless mankind hurries outward, ever
to its inventing, under the indeterminable light.

THINKING OF TU FU I REMEMBER WALLACE STEVENS

Et Tu, bureaucrat, fellow traveler upon
    the disinterested harmonium
Reminder of the Emperor, now suggest to the people
    their dutiful responsibilities
Move left, move right, the mountain yields to the cloud
    the will to many voices
It is a horizontal evasion, Huxley says,
    a granite whim fringed by uncomprehending fears
Shifting the complaint but not the ground
    of the complaint
Altering the mode but not the base

Whereas another can sit in an office
    Tu, as you could not
At ease among the flowery flutings of his harmonium
    composing by the stream of peace
Boating under the passional lanterns
    always to a mistuning, a subtle
But audible beating of discordance.
    Ponderous, sublimely

Horizoned sculptures fade to mauve
    through red infernal
Many miles offer many sorrows
    more space is behind closed shutters
A calm room looking out upon bamboo divisions
    the night trembling with frogs
A falling together of impalpable transferences
    cool dew out of an airy substance
"A good life upon very little livelihood."

LETTER TO THE POET THOMAS McGRATH, AFTER HIS COMING TO MY HOUSE FOR A SHORT VISIT IN THE EVENING

You came into the garden while I was reading at the harpsichord.
From the slope below the house
you heard plainly the old-fashioned tinkling pluck
of the quills, like painted breaking glass.
The darkening pine tree bough lay on the window.
Descending and climbing the steep rock paths,
you enquiring of flowers and she answering for them,
we three came together in the overlooking room
where we sat talking of poetry and criticism.
Neither the full cup nor the overturned cup fell between us,
nor persuading, nor explaining.
When the early evening ended we had agreed to exchange poems.

LIKE A COW A DEER'S PATH

These long Saturday afternoons
after you come, before you come, waiting for you to come
across the steep slope from clavier to typewriter
traveling like a cow a deer's path

and come why not often not
leaving me emptying my jug of time, my water colorless glass
variations at the keyboard, the piano, spinet
directionless tail-swishing cud

waiting for you to come
for whom the prophet held up a finger
the absurd romantic wore a velvet coat
freedmen of your abandon preferred exile

prisoner of churches and of psychology
dungeoned under a St Peter Paul of explanations
economically and educationally rationed
you have no body before law

waiting and wondering for you I tell myself fictions
of what may happen when you do come, stanza upon stanza
chapter upon chapter, clarity upon felicity
hidden in what house of me and why so hidden

why
do you not come!

THIS MORNING NO MOON
For Melissa

This morning no moon.
Beyond my glass screens
night and day, sun and shadow
divide the colored city.
The lazy branches of the great pine
separate me from distance.
In this design of depth, accident
of nature overlaying roofs of man,
beauty comes as one sees
and before thinking.

WRITTEN IN A COPY OF HERMAN MELVILLE'S PIERRE

Here, sir, good friend, you have my globular soul
In a reed basket, in the garden of a queen.
You will find me on the river.
Comings and goings should be as brief as possible.
I speak of nothing large.
That damned whale took the ocean.

SPINOZA

At my age Spinoza died
knowing all a man need know,
ascetic, incorruptible
and in every sentence true.

The sum of facts will not be one
nor the precession of all abbots.
Dungeon, faggot, cross, and knout
cannot direct one sentence true.

The reverend and the learned, who
garner the velvets with their quarrels,
a high-tailed hierarchy of squirrels,
preside upon the limb of state.

Their book, tradition, preference,
their benediction, or award
assert the claim of reputation,
assume the portents of their law.

But each one one may be, though how
Spinoza did not tell, the voice
of knowledge incorruptible:
and he is in himself that choice.

A CONCEIT FOR STRAVINSKY

Seldom do I consult the score
to tell in music where I've been.
I score it by the mind's relief,
which thus restoring reads belief,
and in believing hears, a score
of years, those facts that soar.

And fated though one be to see
occurrences' presented grief,
each interval by less or more
detaches from the parent mould
and winged of human thought is bold
to bring me where I wish to be.

For when such intervals combine,
defying gravity and grace,
to press accustom out of line,
spring thought where empty beauty was
and by decision imprint space,
then music's human and made fit for praise.

Some build by tooth, with tail and claw;
you by the eager breath and resonant law.

Tragedy is the soul's release
that by a stage climbs nearer peace;
but music, though a floor the less,
climbs higher and is yet no place.

St Mark the briefest Gospel wrote,
with less of fashion than of note.
Five domes in Venice honor him:

under each you have set a stage
for tragedy, purged of its rage,
five praises concerting one hymn.

They bless who hear, or hearing less
contort, because they cannot bless.
Print shrivels to a light, and they
as crackled shadows twist away.
We are more blest who can restore
through years our taste of your full score.

POETRY, HELL!...

Poetry, hell! like a disease
this making poems for no one to want,
perverted prayer, prophecy, ethic of invective—
like a disease. It's hell!

If word won't live, no one can want it:
you—nor you! Must shape through its shafts like weed
the uncommon common. Everything anybody can do,
that's nothing anybody needs, or needs to do.

Frost on the rime. Poetry! a disease
you learn: cant if it isn't.
Poetry! any talent critic
can posy an edged quilt from an epic of Merlin—
Needle for a sword, Pennyfeather!—
in a cat's-cradle, doves' feet thudding in the woof.

Yet one incanted virgin pinned to Amherst
upon a cloud of unknowing heard the ghosts
of sermons singing hymns, and the iambic
gave gold. She will not be analyzed.

FROM MY WINDOW

From my window
the freshened lamps of the city
flicker below me. Rain
has washed the air clean.
The fabled city in the triangle
between mountains, city within
cities, flashes neon lights
against night. The branch
of the pine tree I do not own
lies across my windows. Nothing
that I see is mine. The tree
grows from my neighbor's garden.
I do not possess my wealth.
Mist steals my view.
A barren moon in the morning
will hang low over radiant hills.

III. *Later Poems*

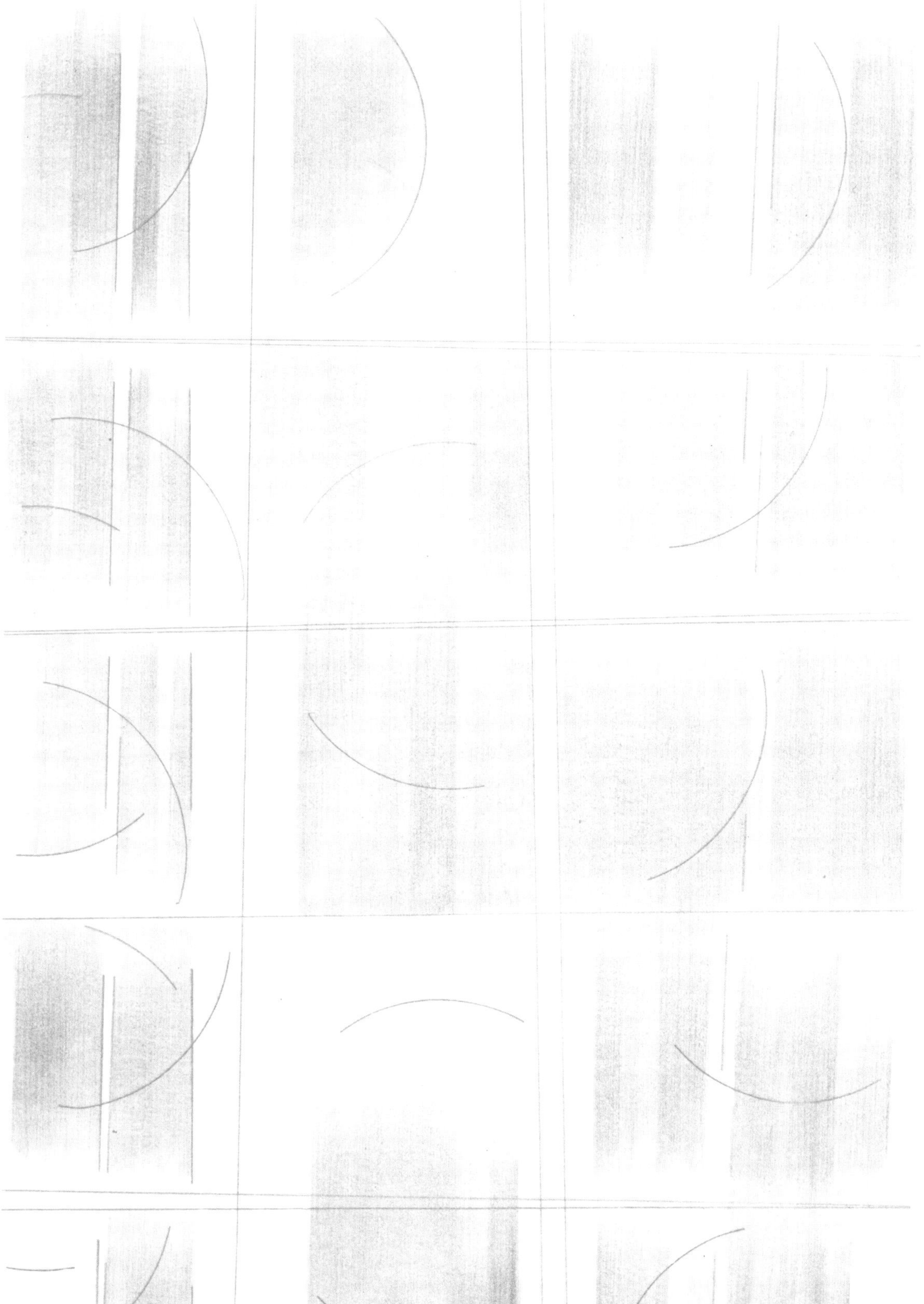

INSCRIBED IN A VOLUME OF MICHELANGELO'S LETTERS

Burned man burning
condemner condemns
any excellent effigy the spirit
ignites

Great arm without shoulder
justice scraped of loveliness
he perishes before the peering
bearded my face

Books   form   beauty
I have willed in that flame
culture to be an eyelash
our faith his scourge

Let the prating praising
public envisage
what they will the face
has been God

The bodiless hand
held him I hold
out my fell.

IF I C

Conceit for Lear

I	INTROIT—the Armed Man, total, IGOR STRAVINSKY	Y
G	Gloria patrem, qualified in excellence, American O K:	K
O	Out of these due, the one man conceiving praiseS	S
R	Responds for multitude, nation and signIFICatioN	N

S	So through one many alike sing unique I	I
T	Toiling, tolling each his mystery in octaV	V
R	Resounding as in Chapel Royal the King's Musick a like A:	A
A	Awe unbelieving that before science the unquenching TigeR	R
V	Vindicates in nakedness all who sign in his sigh T:	T
I	I—but who is he? The reversal reverseS	S
N	Name and nomen, Credo in unam, SIGNificATUR	R
S	Sealed but unseen: that I may go proud, forlorn, O	O
K	K, as in the possession of thy hands, God	G
Y	Yet permitting that I sole serve him in mine I	I

For Igor Stravinsky
after a form proposed by
Lawrence Morton

REMEMBERING OVERLOOKING FEEDING BIRDS OUTSIDE

for hosts recently returned from Japan

To sit stand
contemplating
from your window
the Japanese

aspect branches finches
the ornate cardinal
spouse following at three
paces

to think
composing
the impersonal
voices

out of time tape and NO
history wailing
spectral
drama

to embody the
infinitive
with respect

BEYOND EXCHANGE

Beyond within beyond exchange
dual habitudes

Dis
guarded

myth

d
e s
f a a
i and c
n d r
e e
d d

will will to will

dead hand will rise up from what has been
laying aside Lazarus' napkin

Cassirer heard in a concord of voices
just mythical polyphony

and in a counterpoint empirical
mathematics the logical geometry of the actual

Nobody eats or can add Cezanne apples
or perpetuate
edibelly
alligator pears do
not
Ball and racquet add
up
to
—
collaborate
a complementary
activity
even
among who have condemned the spirit to
extinction

HEIDEGGER WROTE...

HEIDEGGER wrote
BEING

he could not let it be
the sacred
oaks h
a
v
e fallen
only the anthropologist
recalls the macrolith

spirit in split rock spirit through unriven rock
spirit of cave
serve preserve
punish ravish

the 'Big Bang'

neutron and nebula
a moment in universal intelligence

no more than a life

Music spheres no longer downward

Man's own music

another atmosphere

ZOO: IN MEMORY OF THE BLACK GIBBON, BIMBO

There the event, the not to be anticipated
occurs; as among children shouting
will not be consummated; stretches
threatening present:
                                        Bimbo, the black gibbon,
plunging, missing, fallibly
reaching whirls sideway and at rest: unfailing
repertory of an availing, innate ease.

Evolving museum, where the not to be
anticipated occurs, among children shouting:
the inhuman devolving humane friction,
bypassing an iconic selfhood:
                                                        not
its own tailless choristers howling
felicity among boasts of bulging browse:
a new species of idiomatic clarity, at peace.

AUTHORITY

Authority to use
what one does not possess,
to know to do
what one does not believe

The condition is mortal,
but why waste
rest
debating that conclusion

EPITAPH FOR LORINE NIEDECKER

Poems like fieldstones,
not carved but graveled
and weathered to their shape.

MARVELLING ON THE EVE OF MY 65th BIRTHDAY

The universe external runs
coursing amid a blaze of suns,
but the interior phantasm, me,
tho' Ego-eyed I cannot see.

Sixty-five maturing years
peered at through veiling atmospheres:
I cannot reconceive one day
of all which have traversed my way.

Conscience cries at me in derision:
Where, what the object of that vision
your mounted scope would cerebrate?
   Insight unsought, no words might state.

Where are the gardens of your praises,
the hedge-screen shapely of pruned phrases,
the critical opinions
of other men's dominions?

   I did not plant for beds of bloom
   but textures where mind free can roam
   in glance, a casual wilderness
   every season will caress.

   Pitying myself I but repeat
   the failure at the crux of fate:
   in animal ecstasy, to breathe,
   and without that breath, the swath.

   I had a son who could not breathe;
   seven years he lived with death.

Pity he would not take but laughed,
cruelly, at one who looked at him in grief.

In spice and gold of habitude—
Indies' deception New World's truth—
the perennial holds abode
restructured in each age of youth.

I do not hunt the graves of those
I loved: beneath earth nothing stays
but artifact. What lives lies not
in me, so let the Ego rot.

Still behind growth the seeker seeks
one searching self, the unsetting sun,
where sense in desert conscience partakes
and love's fault fails divining unison.

LECTURE: ON THE ROCKS

John Cage writes, he wrote, Now and then I come across an article on that rock garden in Japan where there's just a space of sand and a few rocks in it.

a
In my garden I have sand pool and
an
in other part of my garden there is
a gravel pond.

Not neat nor pious
falling on my gravel pond
twigs, leaves, pine needles.

For Cage there is always the public aspect:

everybody to meditate privately all at once
together

when he met Ashihara,

the Japanese music and dance critic, John Cage says, I told him that I doubted whether their relationship was a planned one, that the emptiness of the sand was such that it could support stones at any points in it.

Daily monks weed, rake

gravel ocean where

tourists contemplate silence.

Ashihara had already given Cage a present (some table mats); now he gave him a necktie.

Is one to interpret this that the westernized Japanese
critic gave of his own stock a peculiarly Western object.

Not a question but a statement.

Cage opposes rocks with sand.

The sand is not empty; the gravel ocean is not empty;

reverberant with the rocks the garden responds.

Each stone is as perfectly shaped as a grain of sand; has meaning like a word where it is placed; becomes a renewed atmosphere in every light and profile.

Pruned pittosporum branches

of the hedge I trim

cleared of their weight of

leafage bound the upper garden.

These do not influence
catch the sight

the visual artists who visit me: tourists

in the visual see the current preconceptions.
good at it

To be an artist may be to see only the current preconceptions.

with the Indians
Instead of in the Heavenly Kingdom Wm. Penn signing the Treaty.

re
Believing they a free of the conceptual they do not see
the bared, bending limbs of the hedge.

One would have to say to them: See how like the Dancers

of Matisse

these perpetually dance.
The bared limbs dance.

Each year in late autumn renewing their perpetual dance

in the first month of winter carefully directing it with my

clippers

A Japanese gardener stops his truck and looks.

One visiting told me I should prune the potocarpus Japanese fashion.

I said, No, it isn't a Japanese
garden.
It is this garden.

I did not say to him, I am not a tourist.

Anything should not be anywhere. Anything

should be where it is not anywhere else.

Not to be original.

An object. A statement. An object in itself.

A statement is a basis of discussion and does not depend

on proof. An object means what it is.

Not separate from the

reverberance

of being where it is

To place is to set in motion.

Esthetically

Ecstatically

To place is to say that this action

changes the atomic clock.

That is to convey meaning. What is it is that what it is.

It does not communicate.

To communicate is to invite *you* to receive *my* message.

Therefore conceptual: therefore the Dancers

of Matisse dance in my hedge.

I do not prune my hedge to resemble the

Dancers of Matisse.

The hedge
would not be a work of art in a
museum.

Unlike Duchamps' shovel
Rauschenberg's goat

every day it changes by growing.

Painted it might become that. Photographed, liberated

from background, kerbs, poles, houses, roofs, parked

automobiles it might become that.

What?

This
Not a message now
this

Lillian Steuber, the pianist, walking in the dark garden, felt

the reverberance, saw
after dark the melody of the pruned hedge.

By what right is it my hedge?
It is not any other hedge.

I do not possess my wealth.

Breathe silence, night

hollow breath fluttering bamboo

bird in snow branches
[From the tape he made for me the late master Nyodo Jin plays the bamboo flute.]

One does not preserve the strict form

one does not possess form

of a rock in the garden.

The strict form is where it is.

One blue rock from the beach

stands in my garden in the absolute shape

of a Madonna and Child

white
a thin strip of quartz accentuating the enclosing arm

before a shrine of one rock, blasted, I found by the roadside

lighted by a white begonia and violets.

Accident conceptualized in the library of the spirit.

I believe in chance, not prepared chance.

REVELATION

Open any book it will be the oracle you wish.

But Croesus! you must read the answer.

The dotty hero learned too late when he'd had the heat on him.

AUTHORITY

In what it proceeds from, final.

In itself—the object, the occasion, oneself bearing it.

In use—knowledge.

The triune, the Trinity, that all think masculine.

Opposed to it the conceptual, the Madonna, feminine.

The stone untroubled because passing dogs use it.

by accident in nature it bears by accident a message no less shaped by accident in nature because it bears in nature a message no less shaped by nature in accident it bears a message shaped in nature no less

Angel vertical over the threshold

on a breathing of wingtips,
perspective opening through into unstaged gardens,
eyes a plotless real:
you will not parley
reasoning with me, only the weather
of an intermediate report,
held here in a silence
before the rustling before the storm.

I ask the New York critic: Have you slaughtered a pork-chop?
In periodical addicts bestrays edicts of vogue blague hip not hep.
Art is forever the rediscovery that is not in fashion.

By the folds of your garments
I know you are not substantial,
invisible as when mountains tremble,
breeze crossing the surfaces of waves,
not a painter's dimensions:

Art is at first the pathetic outcry of a personal soul, we think.

if you hang there hovering,

you must be in the second

person singular, presence

without fault, without feeling, without fate.

The first art is vatic, spiritual business of a group.
Who sets down in no matter.

Didn't get past Dante.
Blake tired remind us.

You are the voice—you are a voice—

and have said nothing I can know.

In your translucent amber no thought gazes:

myself, thinly reflected,

hovering above a destination:

So then after that art returned to being the
pathetic outcry

of a unique person, we think.

A progressing curriculum of disorder.

Genius ambition masterpiece—ambitious masterpieces

Diablo, solitaire, the Once of Ones!

Seeking rest, chaos, silence
as each one thinks, No thingk

Foppishly alike we believe we do not conform.

Rocks still standing in the same place where they are in the sand garden

Mediate They have not moved.

Hallow our hollows, lies where we have slain.

not
What we know is what we believe; what we believe

is not the information we have; the information
we
is not what we know.
have

HOLLO OUR HALLOWS

The stone fish leaps in the sand pool,

leaves glint to green;

light on the rose mountain on the purple mountain

slides on a snail's track;

and in a moment

all that was monumental has been translated.

BIOGRAPHICAL NOTE

Peter (Bertram) Yates was born November 30th, 1909, in St. Catherine's, Ontario, where his parents had moved from Northern New York. He was educated in Canada and then at Union College and Princeton University where he graduated A.B. in English in 1931. The next year he moved to Southern California where he lived until 1968, and where he and his wife, Frances Mullen Yates, a concert pianist, established and maintained from 1939 to 1954 *Evenings on the Roof*, a concert series which developed a wide reputation for introducing modern music and which still continues under another name. Shortly after this, in 1940, he began writing his series of monthly articles on music and the other arts for *California Arts and Architecture* where he was one of the earliest champions of the music of Ives and also of the later Schoenberg and Stravinsky, and which continued until 1967. Because of these articles he became well known as a critic. All of this was done in his spare time while holding down a full-time job with the California Department of Employment, raising a family of three sons (one of whom, John, died tragically of polio after seven years in an iron lung), much other writing of poetry and prose, frequent lecturing, conducting extensive correspondence with his many friends, and running a series of radio broadcasts in Los Angeles for a number of years.

On his retirement from the California Department of Employment in 1962 he wrote *An Amateur at the Keyboard* (1964), an exploration of the joys of making music for the pleasure of it, and *Twentieth Century Music* (1967), an extensive survey of modern music. In 1968, despite the fact that his only academic credentials were his Bachelor's degree from Princeton, he was offered the position of Chairman of the Music Department at the State University College at Buffalo, New York, and moved back there, where he remained active in teaching and writing on music and the philosophy of criticism until his sudden death in February 1976.